Cockatiels

and Other Parrots

Editor in Chief: Paul A. Kobasa
Supplementary Publications: Christine Sullivan, Scott Thomas
Research: Mike Barr, Cheryl Graham
Graphics and Design: Kathy Creech, Sandra Dyrlund, Tom Evans
Permissions: Loranne K. Shields
Indexing: David Pofelski
Prepress and Manufacturing: Carma Fazio, Anne Fritzinger, Steven Hueppchen,
Writer: Lisa Klobuchar

For information about other World Book publications, visit our Web site at http://www.worldbookonline.com or call 1-800-WORLDBK (967-5325).

For information about sales to schools and libraries, call 1-800-975-3250 (United States); 1-800-837-5365 (Canada).

World Book, Inc.
233 N. Michigan Avenue
Chicago, IL 60601
U.S.A.

Library of Congress Cataloging-in-Publication Data

Cockatiels and other parrots.
    p. cm. -- (World Book's animals of the world)
    Summary: "An introduction to cockatiels and other parrots, presented in a
highly illustrated, question and answer format. Features include fun facts,
glossary, resource list, index, and scientific classification list"--Provided by publisher.
    Includes bibliographical references and index.
    ISBN-13: 978-0-7166-1327-5
    ISBN-10: 0-7166-1327-1
    1. Cockatiel--Miscellanea--Juvenile literature. 2. Parrots--Miscellanea--Juvenile
literature. I. World Book, Inc. II. Series.
SF473.C6C64 2007
636.6'8656--dc22
                        2006016682

World Book's Animals of the World
Set 5: ISBN 978-0-7166-1325-1

Printed in China
2 3 4 5 6 12 11 10 09 08

Picture Acknowledgments: Cover © Arco Images/Alamy Images; © Juniors Bildarchiv/Alamy Images; © John Taylor, Alamy Images; © David Wall, Alamy Images; © ZSSD/SuperStock.

© Arco Images/Alamy Images 3, 17, 31; © image100/Alamy Images 57; © Juniors Bildarchiv/Alamy Images 35; © Norvia Behling 59; © Katrina Brown, Shutterstock 29; © Jorg Carstensen, dpa/Landov 15; © Churchill & Klehr Photography 51; © Gerry Ellis, Minden Pictures 33; © Graeme Teague Photography 53; © Frans Lanting, Minden Pictures 43; © Cyril Laubscher, Dorling Kindersley 5, 7, 25, 45; © Carolyn A. McKeone 19; © Claus Meyer, Minden Pictures 39; © Ulrike Schanz 23; © Jay S. Simon, Getty Images 61; © Volker Steger, SPL/Photo Researchers 49; © age fotostock/SuperStock 37; © ZSSD/SuperStock 41; © John Taylor, Alamy Images 13, 21; © David Wall, Alamy Images 4, 47; © Jorg & Petra Wegner, Animals Animals 27; © David Ziegler 55.

Illustrations: WORLD BOOK illustrations by John Fleck 9.

World Book's Animals of the World

Cockatiels

and Other Parrots

WORLD
BOOK

a Scott Fetzer company
Chicago
www.worldbookonline.com

Contents

What Is a Parrot?

A parrot is a type of colorful, noisy bird. Parrots live in tropical forests and grasslands throughout the world. There are over 350 species (kinds) of parrots.

Parrots range in color from almost pure white to a rainbow of greens, yellows, blues, and reds. The smallest parrots are just about 3 inches (8 centimeters) long. The largest are over 36 inches (91 centimeters) long. But parrots have a few traits (features or characteristics) in common. They have a strong, hooked bill and a thick, muscular tongue. A parrot uses its bill like a hand of sorts, to help it climb among tree branches.

People keep many kinds of parrots as pets because the birds are smart, fun, and able to give and receive affection. One of the most popular parrot pets is the Australian parrot called the cockatiel *(KOK uh TEEL)*. Cockatiels are relatively small-sized parrots. They are about 12 inches (30 centimeters) long. Cockatiels are mostly gray, but the male has a bright yellow head, while the head colors of the female are not as bright.

Cockatiels

What Does a Cockatiel Look Like?

A cockatiel has a long, pointed tail and a crest of feathers on its head. A cockatiel's body is small and lightweight. Cockatiels have feet with two toes pointing forward and two pointing backward. These strong feet enable parrots to grasp fruits and nuts, to climb, and to hang from tree branches.

Cockatiels have a patch of orange on each cheek. The male's cheek patch is a brighter orange than the female's, and the rest of the male's cheek is yellow. In the female, the cheek is mostly gray with a fainter orange cheek patch.

Over years of breeding (mating) cockatiels in captivity (among humans and not in the wild), people have developed different color patterns for cockatiels. Lutino *(loo TEE noh)* cockatiels are a very pale yellow all over and have red eyes. Pied *(pyd)* cockatiels are a patchy gray, yellow, and white. Cinnamon cockatiels are light gray all over with a brownish tinge. Pearl cockatiels have feathers that are either dark with a light border or light with a dark border.

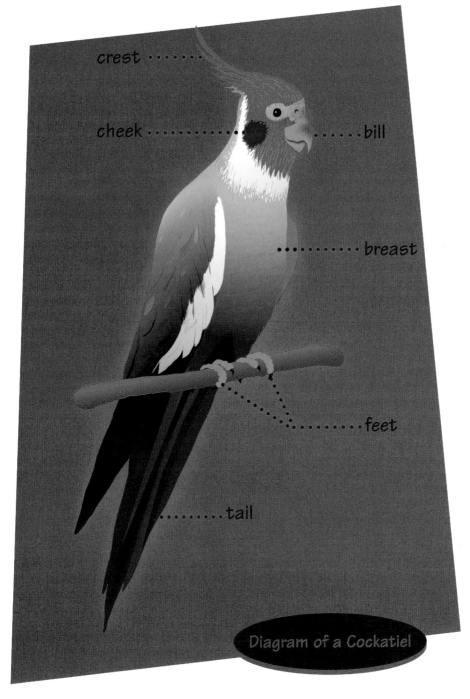

crest ·······

cheek ···················· ······bill

··············· breast

········· feet

·········· tail

Diagram of a Cockatiel

Where Do Cockatiels Live in the Wild?

Cockatiels are native to Australia. Wild cockatiels can be found across the entire Australian continent, though they are now rare along the coastline.

Cockatiels generally live in open spaces. They prefer grassy areas near water. These birds eat seeds, fruit, and berries. Cockatiels also feed in grain fields. They may live in small family groups, but they sometimes gather in large flocks.

Like many other parrots, cockatiels make their nests in holes in trees. They lay their eggs in the soft, decaying wood that collects in the bottom of the hole.

World Map

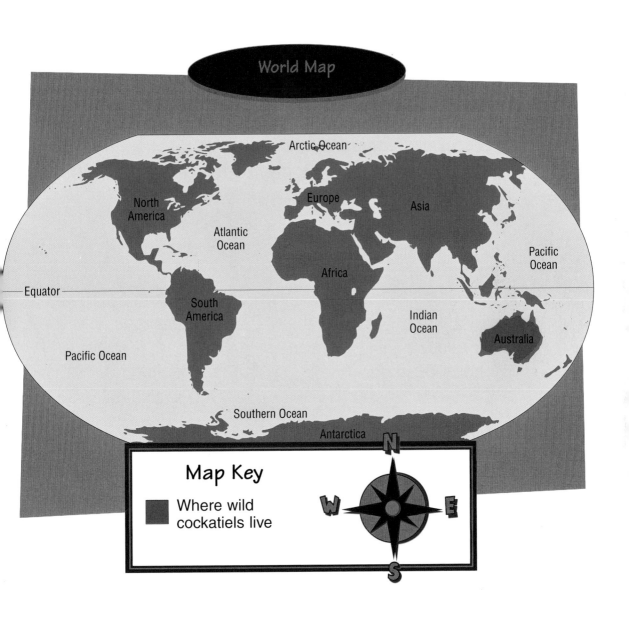

Arctic Ocean

North America

Europe

Asia

Atlantic Ocean

Pacific Ocean

Africa

Equator

South America

Indian Ocean

Pacific Ocean

Australia

Southern Ocean

Antarctica

Map Key

Where wild cockatiels live

N
W E
S

11

What Kind of Personality Might a Pet Cockatiel Have?

A cockatiel's personality depends on the individual. Some cockatiels may be bold and active. These birds might play energetically and explore their surroundings. Other cockatiels may spend more time sitting quietly on a perch or on the shoulder of a trusted person. Some cockatiels might be friendly with strangers. Others may allow only favorite family members to touch them. Some cockatiels enjoy gentle petting and caressing. Others do not like being touched.

As a rule, hand-fed cockatiels (those raised by people) are tame and gentle if treated properly. These birds are usually calm, and they do not make annoying, shrieking calls unless they are frightened. They tend to be affectionate and gentle, even with small children. They may, however, have a strong need for attention.

Most cockatiels love to whistle, and some may learn to say a few words.

12

A cockatiel perching on a friend

What Should You Look for When Choosing a Cockatiel?

The cockatiel you choose should be fully weaned, or able to eat on its own. This usually happens by the time a bird is 7 or 8 weeks old.

To make sure you get a healthy bird, look for smooth, clean-looking feathers and bright eyes. Make sure the eyes are not runny, the bill is dry, and that the vent (opening at the end of the digestive tract) is clean. Also, make sure the skin on the feet is smooth and not flaky. Healthy cockatiels are lively and active. Do not choose a bird that sits fluffed up in a corner; it may be sick.

The Australian government bans the export of wild cockatiels, so most pet cockatiels are hatched in captivity. You can buy a cockatiel from a pet store or from a private breeder, or you may adopt one from a rescue group (see page 52). No matter where you get your cockatiel, make certain that the place is clean and the birds are well cared for.

Many types of parrots at a pet shop

What Does a Cockatiel Eat?

In the wild, a cockatiel, like other parrots, eats a mostly herbivorous diet (a diet of grasses and other plants). Cockatiels love seeds. But a diet that has only seeds is not healthy for your bird.

Along with seeds, cockatiels should eat a variety of fresh fruits and vegetables. Your cockatiel will also enjoy such healthful human foods as cooked grains and beans, tofu, sprouts, small servings of fish or chicken, and cooked or uncooked pasta.

Cockatiels, like humans, love junk food, and it is just as bad for them as it is for us. Avoid giving your cockatiel potato chips, french fries, and other salty, fatty fried foods.

Never let your cockatiel eat such foods as chocolate, avocados, or coffee. And, make certain the bird is never allowed to drink from glasses that contain alcoholic beverages. All these things could make your bird sick, or even kill it.

Cockatiels eating

17

Where Should a Pet Cockatiel Be Kept?

A pet cockatiel is safest in a cage. A cockatiel's cage should be at least 18 inches (46 centimeters) wide, 16 inches (41 centimeters) deep, and about 18 inches (46 centimeters) tall. The bars of the cage should be less than ½ inch (1.25 centimeters) apart.

The cage should have a few perches—bars, branches, or anything else on which a bird can come to rest—of different shapes and sizes. Such perches help to keep your cockatiel's feet healthy. The cage should have three bowls—one for water, one for dry food, and one for veggies and fruits. Provide safe toys made of plastic or wood. Cockatiels also enjoy mirrors and bells.

Most cages have a grate on the bottom and a tray under the grate. Line the tray with newspapers. The bird's droppings and discarded food will drop through the grate onto the paper. Change the paper every day. Once a week, clean the cage bars with mild soap and water using a small scrub brush.

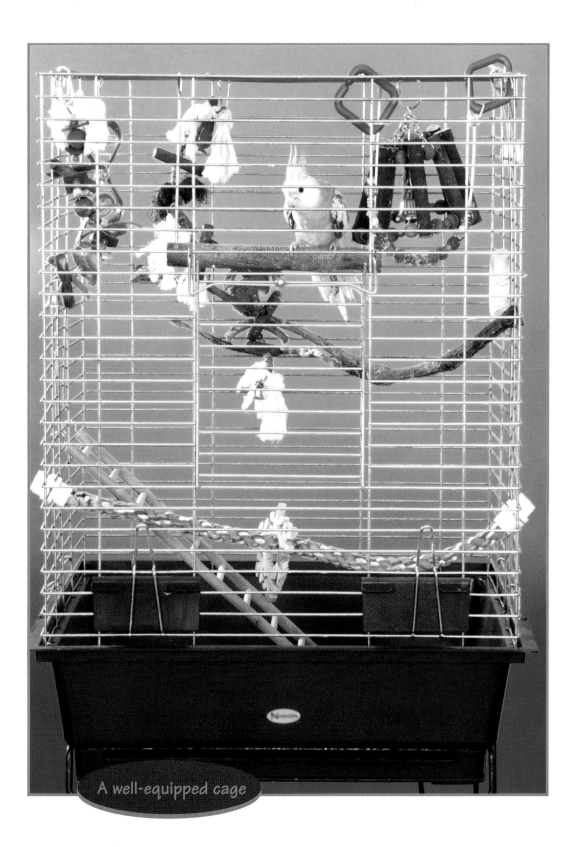

A well-equipped cage

How Does a Cockatiel Groom Itself?

Like other birds, a cockatiel grooms its feathers every day. Feathers are made of hairlike structures, called barbs, which hook together. Through normal activity, the barbs become separated. Cockatiels use their beaks to "zip" the barbs on their feathers back together. This action smoothes the feathers. Smooth feathers are better for flying. Cockatiels also apply oil to their feathers from a gland on their lower back. This grooming of the feathers is called preening.

Birds also remove the cuticle from their new feathers. The cuticle is a papery covering that protects new feathers as they grow. When the feather is fully grown, the cuticle needs to come off. Cockatiels remove the cuticle from new feathers by nibbling that cuticle with their beaks. You can help your cockatiel remove the cuticles from feathers on its head by gently scratching its head with your fingernail. But do not remove the cuticle from a feather that is still growing. That is painful for your bird.

Helping a cockatiel with grooming

21

What About Training a Cockatiel?

A cockatiel may or may not be hand-tamed (used to being handled by humans) when you bring it home. And, even a hand-tamed bird may be shy at first. Approach a shy or untamed bird a little at a time until it learns to trust you. You can start by standing near its cage. If it appears calm, reach into the cage and hold your hand inside there for a few moments.

Some pet stores and breeders teach young cockatiels basic commands before they sell them. If, however, your bird has not learned these commands, you will have to teach them to your pet. One of the first and most important commands to teach your cockatiel is that command which tells your bird to step up onto your hand or finger. Place your finger against the bird's tummy and gently push upward while saying, "step up" or "up." The bird will soon learn to climb up onto your finger. Most cockatiels love to perch on a trusted human, so they usually learn this command quickly.

A cockatiel perching
on a friend's finger

Can Cockatiels Talk?

Yes, some cockatiels can talk a little. Males usually talk more than females.

You can train your cockatiel to talk by repeating simple phrases to it in a clear voice. Cockatiels can also learn to say words and phrases on their own if they hear them every day.

But even if your cockatiel does not talk, it has ways of expressing its feelings. Your cockatiel's crest says a lot about how the bird is feeling. The crest may lie flat against the head with only the tip curling up. This means the bird is relaxed. When your cockatiel raises its crest up, it is busy or interested in something. If your bird is upset, it may point its crest forward and stretch its neck.

A cockatiel with its crest raised

What Kinds of Exercise or Play Are Needed?

Flying can be considered both exercise and play for a bird. But you will have to decide whether to have your bird's wings clipped in order to hinder the bird's flying or to allow it to fly. "Clipping" involves trimming feathers on the animal's wings. It does not hurt the animal. If you decide to have your pet's wings clipped, ask your vet to clip them for you.

A bird with clipped wings can fly only a few feet. This makes it less likely that a bird could escape through a door or open window. Once you clip your cockatiel's wings, however, you may need to help your bird get exercise. Do this by letting it perch on your finger and gently raising and lowering your arm. The bird will flap its wings as it moves up and down.

A cockatiel has many other ways of playing besides flying. Cockatiels also like to chew and nibble and to climb and swing. Most cockatiels also really like baths and showers. They enjoy stretching their wings while being spritzed with a spray bottle.

A cockatiel taking
a "shower"

How Do Cockatiels Care for Their Young?

A female cockatiel, or hen, lays 2 to 9 eggs. The hen and her mate—a male cockatiel, or cock—take turns sitting on their eggs. In 18 to 21 days, the chicks (young birds) hatch from these eggs. Newly hatched cockatiels are covered with soft, yellow feathers called down.

The parents feed the chicks with a thick liquid that they bring up from their crop. The parents feed the chicks for about 40 days. Toward the end of this 40-day period, the parents begin to feed the chicks less and less. The chicks begin to learn to eat on their own. After 7 to 8 weeks, the young birds are able to eat and drink independently of their parents.

Pet cockatiels can have young, as long as they have suitable nesting areas in which to lay eggs and raise chicks.

One-week-old
cockatiel chicks

How Can You Keep Your Cockatiel Safe?

Cockatiels are active and curious, which means they can get into all kinds of trouble in their home. Here are some tips for protecting your cockatiel from dangers:

- Never leave your bird alone with other pets.

- Birds are very sensitive to chemicals in the air. Do not let your pet breathe in fumes from household cleaners, candles, or air fresheners. Keep your bird out of the kitchen when someone is cooking there.

- Be careful about what kinds of plants you grow in your home. Some plants can be poisonous to small birds.

- Be extra watchful about open doors and windows if your bird can fly. A pet can easily escape.

A cockatiel explores
its surroundings

Who Are the Cockatiel's Parrot Relatives?

The cockatiel's closest parrot relative is the cockatoo. A cockatiel is, in fact, a kind of mini cockatoo. Cockatoos are a family of large, crested birds. They range in size from around 12 to 29 inches (30 to 74 centimeters) high. Cockatoos live in Australia and parts of Southeast Asia. Some types of cockatoos are white, and these birds may have yellow, pale pink, peach, or orange in their crests and under their wings. Other cockatoos, called palm cockatoos, are black. Rose-breasted cockatoos, or galahs, are gray and pink.

Australia is the original home of another parrot related to the cockatiel—budgerigars *(buhj uhr ee GAHRZ)*, also known as budgies or parakeets (see page 34).

Other relatives include Amazons (see page 38), gray parrots, lories and lorikeets (see page 46), lovebirds (see page 36), macaws (see page 40), and pocket parrots (see page 42).

A cockatoo

Which Is the Most Popular Parrot Pet?

Budgies (budgerigars), which are one of the types of birds that are also called parakeets, are by far the most popular parrot pet. Budgies are originally from Australia. They were first brought to Europe in the mid-1800's, and they soon became quite popular. Budgies are beautiful and gentle. They are small, so they don't need a lot of space, and they are very inexpensive to buy and care for. Budgies can become very good talkers.

The natural coloring of the budgie was green with a yellow head and blue-edged feathers along the back. But breeders have developed budgies in many other colors, including yellow, blue, white, and cinnamon.

Budgies

Which Is the Most "Romantic" Parrot?

The most "romantic" parrots are lovebirds. Many types of lovebirds choose a mate and keep that mate for life. But there are other kinds of birds—swans, for example—that often mate for life, and we don't call them lovebirds. Lovebirds earned their common name because of the affection mating lovebirds show their partners. A pair of mating lovebirds will often sit very close to each other and might spend hours each day caressing one another with their bills. The male may also feed his mate. These birds are so associated with cuddling that when a human couple behaves in an affectionate matter, we sometimes call them "lovebirds."

You might think that pet lovebirds can only be kept in pairs. Although lovebirds are very social, it is not necessary to keep a pair. In fact, if only one bird is kept, it will probably form a closer bond to its keeper.

36

Lovebirds

Who Is an Opera Singer?

Amazons are a group of parrots native to Latin America and some Caribbean islands. Yellow-headed Amazons are especially famous for their singing. Many of these birds have been known to learn songs from operas, called arias *(AH ree uhz),* but ordinarily they make up their own words and tunes for the songs they sing.

Amazons are mostly green, short-tailed, chunky birds that are also known for their excellent talking abilities. Common Amazon pet species include the yellow-headed (also called double yellows), yellow-naped, orange-winged, red-lored, blue-fronted, mealy, and lilac-crowned. Some of the best talkers among this group are the yellow-headed and the yellow-naped Amazons.

Amazons are bold, noisy, playful, acrobatic, and curious. They have a reputation for taking a strong like or dislike to certain people.

Amazon parrots

Which Kind of Parrot Is the Largest?

The largest parrots are macaws. These long-tailed parrots measure from 12 to 39 inches (30 to 100 centimeters) long. Macaws are big, bold, colorful birds, with personalities to match. The macaw is the parrot most commonly associated with pirates in films.

Macaws are native to forested areas of South America and Mexico. They have become rare in the wild, however. Several macaw species are endangered (in danger of extinction, or dying out).

Macaws are easily tamed, but they are not as common a pet as other types of parrots. Macaws are large, they scream very loudly, and they may bite. People tend to choose smaller and more manageable parrots for pets.

A macaw

Who Hides in a Pocket?

Brotogeris *(broh toh JAIR uhs)* parrots and parrotlets are tiny parrots from Latin America. Both kinds of birds are called pocket parrots because of their small size and because they like to tuck themselves into pockets and other small spaces. Even though these parrots are small, they have all the personality of larger parrots.

Popular types of Brotogeris parrots include canary-winged parakeets, orange-chinned parakeets, and gray-cheeked parakeets. Members of this genus are feisty, playful birds. They do, however, have loud and raspy voices.

Unlike Brotogeris parrots, parrotlets are quiet birds that seldom screech. Parrotlets instead prefer to make sweet-sounding chirps.

A Brotogeris parrot
eating flowers

43

Who Looks Really Different?

The males and females of most parrot species do not look very different from one another. The two actually look quite alike.

There is one type of parrot species, though, in which the males and females look completely different. When these birds were first discovered, scientists thought the males and females were two different species of bird. When scientists discovered that these birds were of the same species, they named the species eclectus, which means "made up of a variety of characteristics."

Eclectus parrots are from Australia, New Guinea, and Southeast Asia. The males are bright green with touches of red and blue on the wings and an orange-yellow upper beak. The females are brilliant red, blue, and purple, with a black beak.

Male (left) and female (right) eclectus parrots

Which Parrots Have a "Brush" in Their Mouth?

Parrots called lories and lorikeets feed on a diet of flower nectar (a sugary liquid produced by flowering plants) and pollen (yellowish powder formed in the male organs of flowers). The tongues of these birds have tiny, fingerlike growths—something like a brush—at the tip. These growths help the birds to lap up nectar. In captivity, lories and lorikeets need a partially liquid diet to replace their natural nectar diet.

People like to keep lories and lorikeets as pets because they are playful and acrobatic. Some are also good talkers. And, some lories and lorikeets are quite beautiful, with incredible combinations of colors.

Lorikeets

47

How Smart Are Parrots?

Parrots are among the smartest of animals. Parrots are about as intelligent as dolphins and primates (other than people). Parrot experts describe the intelligence of a large parrot as being about the same as that of a 3- to 5-year-old child. And, for parrots the size of African grays and Amazons, all this power is packed into a brain the size of a walnut. Parrots' love of play, their curiosity, and their ability to respond to their caregivers' emotions are some of the ways we can see the intelligence of these birds.

Parrots that talk can use words and phrases as though they know their meaning. For example, a parrot may say "Time for dinner!" when its caregiver is bustling around the kitchen. Or it may ask for tickles or its favorite treat. Some parrots are expert engineers. They can unlock cage doors and take apart complicated toys with their beaks.

Researchers are trying to train parrots to interact with a computer. One day, perhaps, a parrot will surf the Internet and play video games while it waits for its owner to get home.

A researcher training a
parrot on a computer

49

What Happens to Pet Parrots That Escape into the Wild?

Pet parrots sometimes escape. And, parrot owners sometimes purposely let their pets loose when they no longer want to care for them. Some of these lost or abandoned pets survive and live in the wild once again.

Animals that were once tame or that are descended from animals that were once tame but that now live in the wild are called feral. So, these parrots are called feral parrots.

Most feral parrot flocks live in warm places, such as southern California and Florida. Flocks have, however, formed in colder places, as well. Flocks of monk, or Quaker, parrots live in Brooklyn, New York; Connecticut; and in Chicago's Hyde Park neighborhood. Monk parrots are able to live through the cold winters because they build large nests of twigs that allow them to stay warm.

50

Monk parrots in a nest in Chicago

Who Takes Care of Pet Parrots That No One Wants?

Parrots can be fun, funny, smart, active, loyal, and affectionate pets. But they are not for everyone. They can be messy and noisy. They may chew up furniture or other valuable objects in the house. They can be mean to people they don't like. And, they may demand more attention than a person is able to give. Unhappy parrots sometimes develop bad habits. They may scream constantly or pull out their feathers. Faced with these problems, people may no longer want to keep their parrots.

Bird-rescue organizations take in unwanted, abused, and neglected parrots. Such organizations try to find new homes for unwanted parrots. Many such parrots can return to health and happiness in a good home. Sadly, though, some neglected or abused birds develop severe emotional or mental problems. Many rescue organizations also try to provide a permanent, caring home for birds that are not fit for adoption to the public.

A parrot sanctuary in Honduras

53

What Is a Bird Show Like?

Bird clubs sponsor shows where pet birds are judged. Both the National Cockatiel Society and the American Cockatiel Society Web sites (see page 64) offer a lot of information on showing your bird.

Start months in advance to prepare your bird for a show. Make sure you feed your pet the best possible diet. Bathe your bird every day to keep its feathers smooth, glossy, and waterproof. To bathe a bird, place about 1 inch (2.5 centimeters) of cool water in a shallow dish or pie plate. Place the bird in the water. Your cockatiel will splash around and give itself a bath. Allow its feathers to air dry.

You will also have to train your bird so it will be calm and well behaved during judging. Get your pet used to being in a show cage. This type of cage has three sides that are solid, while the fourth side, placed at the front, has bars that allow your bird to be seen by the judge. Put your bird into the cage for a little while every day and slowly increase the amount of time it spends there. Allow your cockatiel to get used to strangers by allowing people that your cockatiel does not know to approach its cage.

A bird show

What Are
Some Common Signs of
Illness in Parrots?

Parrots are very hardy, but they can get sick. With some illnesses, a parrot may not give any signs that it is feeling unwell. With other illnesses, a sick parrot may be less active. It may hide its head in its feathers or fluff them out. If your pet bird changes its behavior for no apparent reason, take it to the vet.

Parrots get mild illnesses, such as infections or intestinal ailments. A bird with a slight infection may have a moist bill.

Signs of serious illness in parrots include changes in the appearance or smell of the droppings, loss of appetite, sneezing, or fluid coming from the eyes and nostrils. Sometimes, by the time such signs of illness appear, it is too late to save the bird. A yearly veterinary examination, therefore, is especially important for parrots.

Budgies at a vet's office

What Routine Veterinary Care Is Need?

Most experts advise cockatiel owners to take their bird to a veterinarian once a year for a checkup. Cockatiels, like most other birds, do not always show signs of illness. A yearly checkup allows a vet to spot diseases that your bird may have. Many illnesses can be treated and cured by your vet if they are discovered early enough.

During an office visit, the veterinarian will look at your cockatiel's body. The vet will examine its eyes, nostrils, and throat. He or she will feel the bird's chest to make sure the animal is not too skinny or too fat. The vet will also check the bird's vent to make sure it is clean. The vet may also take lab tests. For example, he or she may take a sample from your bird's throat with a cotton swab. Such samples can be examined for signs of infection. Finally, a tiny bit of blood might be taken from a bird. This sample, once tested, can show the levels of many substances in the blood. All of these lab tests are done to determine the overall health of your bird.

A veterinarian examining a cockatiel

What Are Your Responsibilities as an Owner?

Smaller parrots, such as cockatiels and budgies, may live about as long as cats and dogs—that is, anywhere from 8 to 15 years. Some small parrots may live for much longer. Basic care for these birds includes providing a healthy diet; clean water; a clean, safe, roomy cage; plenty of attention; and a yearly checkup by a veterinarian.

Larger parrots, such as African grays, Amazons, cockatoos, and macaws come with some additional responsibilities. Larger parrots are often smarter and more demanding than the smaller parrots. A responsible owner of a large parrot teaches the bird how to get along with humans. The bird must be taught not to scream for attention, not to bite, and how to amuse itself while it is alone.

Bigger parrots can also live a very long time— 50 years or more. The owner of a large parrot is responsible for making arrangements for the bird's care in case something happens to him or her.

A cockatiel with friends

61

Parrot Fun Facts

→ One famous flock of feral parrots lives in an area of San Francisco called Telegraph Hill. These parrots, mostly red-masked parakeets (also called cherry-headed conures), were the subject of a 2003 movie titled *The Wild Parrots of Telegraph Hill.*

→ The seventh president of the United States, Andrew Jackson, had a pet parrot. It had to be removed from President Jackson's funeral service because it was calling out naughty words in a very loud voice.

→ The kakapo is a flightless parrot of New Zealand. They come out only at night. They are also the heaviest parrot, tipping the scales at up to 9 pounds (4 kilograms).

→ A macaw can close its beak with a force of about 500 pounds per square inch (35 kilograms per square centimeter). Compare this to the footstep of a three-ton (2,722-kilogram) elephant, which presses on the ground with a force of about 75 pounds per square inch (5.3 kilograms per square centimeter).

Glossary

barb A hairlike branch on the shaft of a bird's feather.

bill The horny part of the jaws of a bird.

captivity In animals, living under the care of humans and not in the wild.

cheek The side of a bird's face, below either eye.

chick A young bird, especially one still in the egg or just hatched.

cock A male bird.

crest A tuft or comb of feathers on the top of a bird's head.

crop A baglike swelling in a bird's digestive tract, before the stomach, where food is stored. Birds sometimes store food for their young in the crop.

feral An animal that has reverted from being domesticated (tamed) to the original wild or untamed state.

hatch In birds, to bring forth (young) from an egg or to emerge from an egg.

hen A female bird.

herbivorous A diet of grasses and other plants.

parakeet A general name for many kinds of small- to medium-sized parrots, especially those with long, pointed tails.

perch A bar, branch, or anything else on which a bird can come to rest.

preening In birds, the smoothing or arranging of their feathers.

trait A feature or characteristic particular to an animal or breed of animals.

tropical An animal or plant that lives in (or comes from) regions near Earth's equator. These regions have mostly warm temperatures year around and plentiful rainfall.

vent In birds and some other animals, the opening at the end of the digestive tract.

Index

(**Boldface** indicates a photo, map, or illustration.)

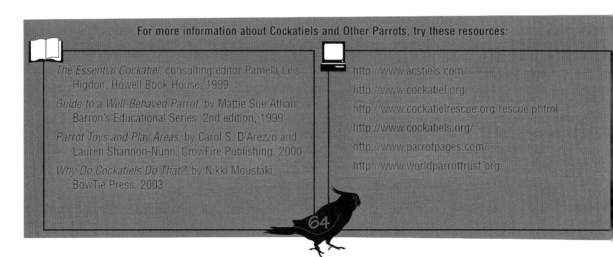

For more information about Cockatiels and Other Parrots, try these resources:

The Essential Cockatiel, consulting editor Pamela Leis Higdon, Howell Book House, 1999

Guide to a Well-Behaved Parrot, by Mattie Sue Athan, Barron's Educational Series, 2nd edition, 1999

Parrot Toys and Play Areas, by Carol S. D'Arezzo and Lauren Shannon-Nunn, CrowFire Publishing, 2000

Why Do Cockatiels Do That?, by Nikki Moustaki, BowTie Press, 2003

http://www.acstiels.com/
http://www.cockatiel.org/
http://www.cockatielrescue.org/rescue.phtml
http://www.cockatiels.org/
http://www.parrotpages.com/
http://www.worldparrottrust.org/

Parrot Classification

Scientists classify animals by placing them into groups. The animal kingdom is a group that contains all the world's animals. Phylum, class, order, and family are smaller groups. Each phylum contains many classes. A class contains orders, an order contains families, and a family contains genuses. One or more species belong to each genus. Each species has its own scientific name. (The abbreviation "spp." after a genus name indicates that a group of species from a genus is being discussed.) Here is how the animals in this book fit into this system.

Animals with backbones and their relatives (Phylum Chordata)
Birds (Class Aves)
True birds (Subclass Neornithes)
Parrots and their relatives (Order Psittaciformes)

Parrots and their relatives (Family Psittacidae)
  Cockatiels (Subfamily Nymphicinae)
    Cinnamon, Lutino, Pearl,
      and Pied cockatiel .... *Nymphicus hollandicus*
  Cockatoos* (Subfamily Cacatuinae)
    Rose-breasted cockatoo (galah) .... *Eolophus roseicappillus*
    Palm cockatoo .... *Probosciger aterrimus*
  Lories and lorikeets (Subfamily Lorinae)   *Chalcopsitta* spp., *Charmosyna* spp.,
                                        Eos spp.,*Glossopsitta* spp., *Lorius* spp.,
                                        Neopsittacus spp., *Oreopsittacus arfaki*,
                                        Phigys solitarius, *Pseudeos fuscata*,
                                        Psitteuteles spp., *Trichiglossus* spp., *Vini* spp.
  Owl Parrots (Subfamily Strigopinae)
    Kakapo .... *Strigops habroptilus*
  True parrots (Subfamily Psittacinae)
    Lovebirds .... *Agapornis* spp.
    Blue-fronted Amazon .... *Amazona aestiva*
    Orange-winged Amazon .... *Amazona amazonica*
    Yellow-naped Amazon .... *Amazona auropalliata*
    Red-lored Amazon .... *Amazona autumnalis*
    Mealy Amazon .... *Amazona farinosa*
    Lilac-crowned Amazon .... *Amazona finschi*
    Yellow-headed Amazon .... *Amazona oratrix*
    Macaws .... *Anodorhynchus* spp., *Ara* spp., *Cyanopsitta spixii*
    Red-masked parakee .... *Aratinga erythrogenys*
    Orange-chinned parakee .... *Brotogeris jugularis*
    Gray-cheeked parakee .... *Brotogeris pyrrhopterus*
    Canary-winged parakee .... *Brotogeris versicolurus*
    Eclectus parrot .... *Eclectus roratus*
    Parrotlet .... *Forpus* spp., *Touit* spp., *Nannopsittaca* spp.
    Budgerigar .... *Melopsittacus undulatus*
    Monk, or Quaker, parrot .... *Myiopsitta monachus*
    African gray parrot .... *Psittacus erithacus*

* Some scientists classify the cockatoos into their own scientific family, Cacatuidae, instead of in the parrot family, Psittacidae.

WITHDRAWN

Let's Read About Our Bodies
Conozcamos nuestro cuerpo

Mouth/Boca

Cynthia Klingel & Robert B. Noyed
photographs by/fotografías por Gregg Andersen

Reading consultant/Consultora de lectura: Cecilia Minden-Cupp, Ph.D.,
Adjunct Professor, College of Continuing and Professional Studies, University of Virginia

Weekly Reader.
EARLY LEARNING LIBRARY

For a free color catalog describing Weekly Reader® Early Learning Library's list of high-quality books, call 1-800-542-2595 or fax your request to (414) 332-3567.

Library of Congress Cataloging-in-Publication Data

Klingel, Cynthia.
   Mouth = Boca / by Cynthia Klingel and Robert B. Noyed. — [Bilingual ed.]
     p. cm. — (Let's read about our bodies = Conozcamos nuestro cuerpo)
   Includes bibliographical references and index.
   Summary: A bilingual introduction to the mouth, what it is used for, and how to take care of it.
   ISBN 0-8368-3076-8 (lib. bdg.)
   1. Mouth—Juvenile literature. [1. Mouth. 2. Spanish language materials—Bilingual.]
  I. Title: Boca. II. Noyed, Robert B. III. Title.
  QM306.K554   2002
  611'.31—dc21   2001055088

This edition first published in 2002 by
Weekly Reader® Early Learning Library
330 West Olive Street, Suite 100
Milwaukee, WI 53212 USA

An Editorial Directions book
Editors: E. Russell Primm and Emily Dolbear
Translators: Tatiana Acosta and Guillermo Gutiérrez
Art direction, design, and page production: The Design Lab
Photographer: Gregg Andersen
Weekly Reader® Early Learning Library art direction: Tammy Gruenewald
Weekly Reader® Early Learning Library page layout: Katherine A. Goedheer

Printed in the United States of America

1 2 3 4 5 6 7 8 9 06 05 04 03 02

Note to Educators and Parents

As a Reading Specialist I know that books for young children should engage their interest, impart useful information, and motivate them to want to learn more.

Let's Read About Our Bodies is a new series of books designed to help children understand the value of good health and of taking care of their bodies.

A young child's active mind is engaged by the carefully chosen subjects. The imaginative text works to build young vocabularies. The short, repetitive sentences help children stay focused as they develop their own relationship with reading. The bright, colorful photographs of children enjoying good health habits complement the text with their simplicity to both entertain and encourage young children to want to learn — and read — more.

These books are designed to be used by adults as "read-to" books to share with children to encourage early literacy in the home, school, and library. They are also suitable for more advanced young readers to enjoy on their own.

Una nota a los educadores y a los padres

Como especialista en lectura, sé que los libros infantiles deben interesar a los niños, proporcionar información útil y motivarlos a aprender.

Conozcamos nuestro cuerpo es una nueva serie de libros pensada para ayudar a los niños a entender la importancia de la salud y del cuidado del cuerpo.

Los temas, cuidadosamente seleccionados, mantienen ocupada la activa mente del niño. El texto, lleno de imaginación, facilita el enriquecimiento del vocabulario infantil. Las oraciones, breves y repetitivas, ayudan a los niños a centrarse en la actividad mientras desarrollan su propia relación con la lectura. Las bellas fotografías de niños que disfrutan de buenos hábitos de salud complementan el texto con su sencillez, y consiguen entretener a los niños y animarlos a aprender nuevos conceptos y a leer más.

Estos libros están pensados para que los adultos se los lean a los niños, con el fin de fomentar la lectura incipiente en el hogar, en la escuela y en la biblioteca. También son adecuados para que los jóvenes lectores más avanzados los disfruten leyéndolos por su cuenta.

Cecilia Minden-Cupp, Ph.D., Adjunct Professor,
College of Continuing and Professional Studies, University of Virginia

This is my mouth.

- - - - - - -

Ésta es mi boca.

I can eat with my mouth.

— — — — — — —

Puedo comer con la boca.

I can talk with my mouth.

- - - - - - -

Puedo hablar con la boca.

I can kiss my doll with my mouth.

Puedo besar a mi muñeca con la boca.

I can smile with my mouth.

– – – – – – –

Puedo sonreír con la boca.

My teeth are in my mouth. I brush my teeth every morning and every night.

- - - - - - -

Los dientes están en la boca. Me cepillo los dientes cada mañana y cada noche.

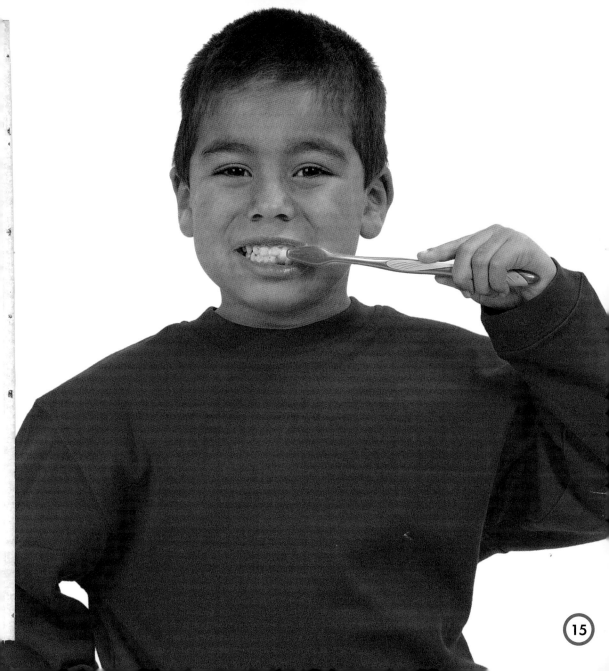

I take care of my mouth.
I go to the dentist.

- - - - - - -

Me cuido la boca.
Voy al dentista.

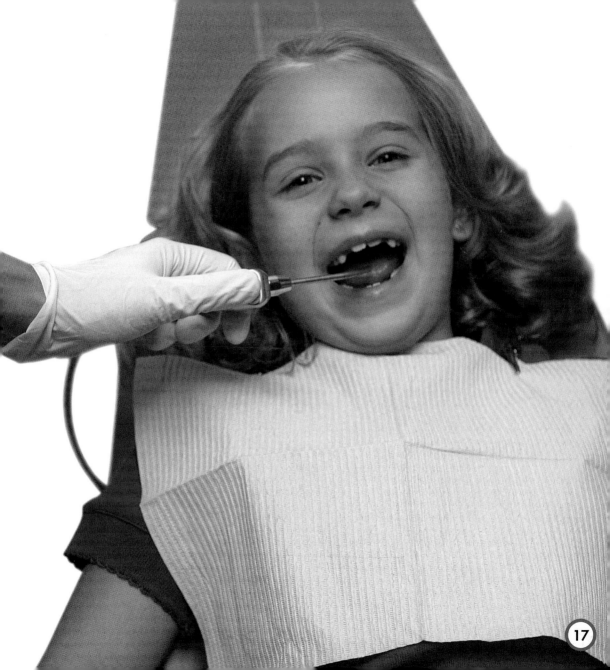

The dentist helps to keep my teeth clean and healthy.

El dentista me ayuda a mantener la boca limpia y saludable.

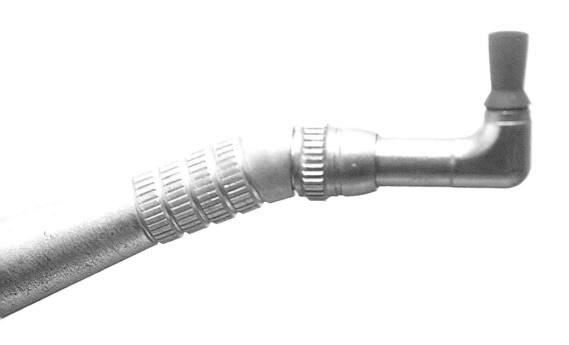

I can make funny faces
with my mouth!

- - - - - - - -

¡Puedo poner caras
divertidas con la boca!

Glossary/Glosario

dentist—a doctor who cares for the teeth and mouth
dentista—médico que cuida los dientes y la boca

healthy—good for the body
saludable—bueno para el cuerpo

teeth—the hard, bony parts of the mouth used to bite and chew
dientes—partes duras y óseas de la boca que usamos para morder y masticar

For More Information/Más información

Fiction Books/Libros de ficción

Faulkner, Keith. *The Wide-Mouthed Frog.* New York:
Dial Books for Young Readers, 1996.

Grohman, Almute, and Patricia Bereck Weikersheimer.
*Dragon Teeth and Parrot Beaks: Even Creatures Brush
Their Teeth.* Carol Stream, Ill.: Quintessence Publishing Co.,
1998.

Nonfiction Books/Libros de no ficción

Moses, Brian. *Munching, Crunching, Sniffling,
and Snooping.* New York: DK Publishing, 1999.

Web Sites/Páginas Web
What Is Spit?

kidshealth.org/kid/talk/yucky/spit.html
To learn why we have saliva in our mouths

Index/Índice

About the Authors/Información sobre los autores

Cynthia Klingel has worked as a high school English teacher and an elementary school teacher. She is currently the curriculum director for a Minnesota school district. Cynthia Klingel lives with her family in Mankato, Minnesota.

Cynthia Klingel ha trabajado como maestra de inglés de secundaria y como maestra de primaria. Actualmente es la directora de planes de estudio de un distrito escolar de Minnesota. Cynthia Klingel vive con su familia en Mankato, Minnesota.

Robert B. Noyed started his career as a newspaper reporter. Since then, he has worked in school communications and public relations at the state and national level. Robert B. Noyed lives with his family in Brooklyn Center, Minnesota.

Robert B. Noyed comenzó su carrera como reportero en un periódico. Desde entonces ha trabajado en comunicación escolar y relaciones públicas a nivel estatal y nacional. Robert B. Noyed vive con su familia en Brooklyn Center, Minnesota.